Cutting-Edge Decoupage

Cutting-Edge Decoupage

30 Easy Projects for Super-Cool Results

Nathalie Mornu

LARK BOOKS

A Division of Sterling Publishing Co., Inc.
New York / London

Senior Editor: Valerie Van Arsdale Shrader

Art Direction: Thom Gaines, Megan Kirby

Cover Designer: Cindy LaBreacht

Assistant Designer: Travis Medford

Art Production Assistant: Jeff Hamilton

Editorial Assistance: Cassie Moore

Editorial Intern: Katrina Usher

Illustration: Travis Medford;
   Orrin Lundgren, page 48

Photographer: Steve Mann;
   additional photography, John Widman,
   pages 67, 68, 89, and 90

Library of Congress Cataloging-in-Publication Data

Mornu, Nathalie.
  Cutting-edge decoupage : 30 easy projects for super-cool results /
Nathalie Mornu. -- 1st ed.
     p. cm.
  Includes index.
  ISBN-13: 978-1-57990-891-1 (hc-plc with jacket : alk. paper)
  ISBN-10: 1-57990-891-8 (hc-plc with jacket : alk. paper)
  1. Decoupage. I. Title.
TT870.M655 2007
745.54'6--dc22
                            2007003620

10 9 8 7 6 5 4 3 2 1

First Edition

Published by Lark Books, A Division of
Sterling Publishing Co., Inc.
387 Park Avenue South, New York, NY 10016

Text © 2007, Lark Books
Photography © 2007, Lark Books
Illustrations © 2007, Lark Books

Distributed in Canada by Sterling Publishing,
c/o Canadian Manda Group, 165 Dufferin Street
Toronto, Ontario, Canada M6K 3H6

Distributed in the United Kingdom by GMC Distribution Services,
Castle Place, 166 High Street, Lewes, East Sussex, England BN7 1XU

Distributed in Australia by Capricorn Link (Australia) Pty Ltd.,
P.O. Box 704, Windsor, NSW 2756 Australia

If you have questions or comments about this book, please contact:
Lark Books
67 Broadway
Asheville, NC 28801
(828) 253-0467

Manufactured in China

ISBN 13: 978-1-57990-891-1
ISBN 10: 1-57990-891-8

For information about custom editions, special sales, premium and corporate
purchases, please contact Sterling Special Sales Department at 800-805-5489 or
specialsales@sterlingpub.com.

Contents

Introduction, 6

Basics, 8

The Projects, 21

Introduction

If you mastered cutting and pasting in grade school—and you undoubtedly did—you can pull off any of the ideas in this book. Decoupage is an incredibly simple way to give objects zing and make them distinctive. The technique is so versatile it can vamp up worn-out, boring items and spice up new ones. Best of all, it's fun and easy. Even a person who's never decoupaged can create terrific-looking stuff. The designers in this book are all experienced crafters, but some had never tried decoupage before. Bet you can't tell seasoned veteran from novice...

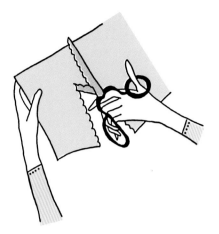

The materials and tools used in decoupage couldn't be simpler: glue, paper, scissors. The technique is elementary, too; you just brush on adhesive to attach a paper cutout. From these humble basics, however, you can achieve astonishingly sophisticated effects. The pieces in this book steer clear of the traditional, elaborate style you might associate with decoupage. The project designers were asked to expand on decoupage's possibilities as a decorative technique, to aim for a clean, modern aesthetic, and to come up with unconventional ideas. They applied not only paper cutouts but restraint, style, wit, and their own sometimes irreverent personalities—and delivered it all with a fresh, updated twist.

You probably won't find the same objects or papers shown here, and that's the whole point. Discover the perfect object—one with great bones—and scout out the perfect paper. Then use the ideas contained in these pages as a departure for creating your own unique stuff. Our designers unearthed the unexpected, working their magic on old windows, vintage-style electric fans, and wooden clothespins. Some bought maps, napkins, or tissue paper to decoupage with, but others came up with inventive techniques for creating one-of-a-kind papers, like bleaching vellum or making color photocopies of fabrics. In a few cases, they splashed the decoupage across both furnishings and walls to weave objects into an environment.

The Basics section includes a brief history of the technique; you join the ranks of some distinguished enthusiasts. You'll also be introduced to the materials and tools used for most of the projects. You're probably familiar with the bulk of them, and, what's better, they're cheap and easy to find.

The 30 projects contain step-by-step instructions packed with helpful tips about techniques, hints on finding just the right images, pointers about tools, or suggestions for variations. Although no project in this book is difficult, we've presented them from simplest to most involved.

As you thumb through the next 90 or so pages, you'll find a collection of decoupage that's a cut above. You may want to rush to get started, but as you take scissors in hand, restrain yourself and remember what you learned in grade school—walk, don't run.

The Basics

Clearly, you have more than a passing acquaintance with cutting and pasting—who doesn't?—but you probably don't know which famous poet was a devotee of decoupage, you could be unaware that decoupage works on plastic, and you may have no idea how to thin paper. Read on.

A SNIPPET OF HISTORY

The term decoupage derives from *découper*, a French word meaning 'to cut out.' The ancient Chinese invented the idea, savvy Venetian businessmen appropriated it after the Renaissance, and eventually royalty was pasting paper cutouts on noble knickknacks. But most of us remember decoupage from the 1960s and 1970s—that most democratic craft resulting in yellowed recipe boxes covered in mushrooms and rec room clocks plastered with unicorns.

Decoupage flourished in mid- to late-18th-century Europe as the result of a craze for *chinoiserie*, fine lacquer work decorated to mimic Chinese or Japanese designs. Venetian painted-furniture guilds made most of this counterfeit lacquer work. At first, artists created designs for master painters to sketch onto furnishings; finally, craftsmen and apprentices filled in color and varnished up to 40 layers sanded to a glossy sheen. Demand was high, consumers wanted the work of the most prestigious artists, and the labor-intensive process took up to a year to finish.

Time is money, right? In an unsurprising move, the industry became more efficient by cutting the middlemen out of the picture. Instead, printers mass-produced artists' designs for apprentices to cut and paste in all sorts of combinations, then finish as before. And so was decoupage invented.

If lowly apprentices had the skill to do it, so might anyone. Travel was arduous, visitors tended to stay for weeks or months, and TV didn't exist yet. Since every lady's sewing kit contained a pair of fine scissors, it was logical to progress from needlework to snipping paper for entertainment. The activity became a pastime for the ordinary person—and the not-so-common one as well.

After its heyday, decoupage waned in and out of fashion, with each era lending its own particular flair. The Victorians, for example, had a fondness for *trompe l'oeil*, using realistic prints and skillfully painted shadows to produce playful optical illusions. What looked like writing implements resting atop a desk, for example, was really just a solid surface. The current revival draws in part on *potichomania*, the mid-19th-century craze for decoupage glued to the underside of clear glass vases.

BLUE-BLOODS OF DECOUPAGE

Madame de Pompadour, the high-powered mistress of Louis XV, was a patron to writers, painters, sculptors, and architects. Perhaps best known for the hairdo named after her, she wasn't a hair cutter, but a paper cutter.

The French queen **Marie Antoinette** and the ladies at her court adored decoupage as a *divertissement*, and by certain accounts they clipped the priceless paintings of Watteau, Boucher, and Fragonard to paste bits onto hatboxes, fans, screens, or any other object they fancied. Off with her head, indeed!

Mary Delaney was a confidante of King George III and Queen Charlotte. At the tender age of 71, she began making incredibly accurate reproductions of plants and flowers cut from tissue paper. See them in the British Museum.

Beau Brummell, the English dandy and pal to a prince regent, took five hours to dress and recommended polishing boots with champagne. Since his servants probably took care of all the chores, he had plenty of time for scissor work.

Between writing exceptional poetry, carrying on scandalous love affairs, world travel, and various military escapades, **Lord Byron** unwound with decoupage. Isn't it delicious to imagine the kind of outrageous imagery he might have snipped?

Queen Victoria not only collected decoupage but also dabbled in it—could it be she began by covering cigar boxes provided by her son, who later became King Edward VII?

In *Running with Scissors,* the memoir of a surreal childhood in the '70s, **Augusten Burroughs's mother**, a delusional and unsuccessful poet but a lady of her times, decoupages the kitchen table with cigarette advertisements, claiming they help her write.

On an episode of *Buffy the Vampire Slayer,* characters discussing the American queen of the domestic arts, **Martha Stewart**, conclude that someone doing that much decoupage must be calling on the forces of darkness.

MATERIALS AND TOOLS

The most important elements for cutting-edge decoupage? Interesting, attractive images, a good imagination, and a strong sense of style. You'll also need a few inexpensive things. You may already own many of them, but if not, they're easy to find. The essentials, of course, are the object you plan to decorate and the paper to do that with. You'll also need a tool to cut the paper, a method for attaching the cutout to your object, and some type of finish to protect your work.

Stalking Your Object
Ah, the thrill of the hunt! Applying decoupage to boxes, clocks, and picture frames is so predictable. Instead, keep your eyes open and your imagination fine-tuned to spot the fabulous and the unexpected. One of our designers, for example, combed the local secondhand stores and flushed out a charming wooden headboard and a cool old suitcase (pages 88 and 52). Another salvaged an abandoned window from a basement to turn into a piece of art (page 83). And one designer had the vision to realize how interesting decoupage would look on the humble clothespin (page 22).

Decoupage can do more than give facelifts to old, shabby objects. We bought many new objects to use in this book. These modern but inexpensive things had a great underlying structure, and we knew that the right cutouts and a little elbow grease would transform them from slightly austere to funky and cool. For example, we liked how colorful, wavy tissue made the cold, contemporary lines of frosted glass lamps feel warm and inviting (page 40).

Wood
Glass
Cardboard
Metal
Porcelain or clay
Stone
Eggshell
Plastic
Cement

Any rigid surface works for decoupage.

Papers

You'll find a boundless array of paper and imagery. Build up a stockpile by saving anything you like. Have you come across a fantastic printed sheet that's in lousy condition? No problem. Iron out the wrinkles on a low setting, making sure to use the appliance on the back side of the sheet.

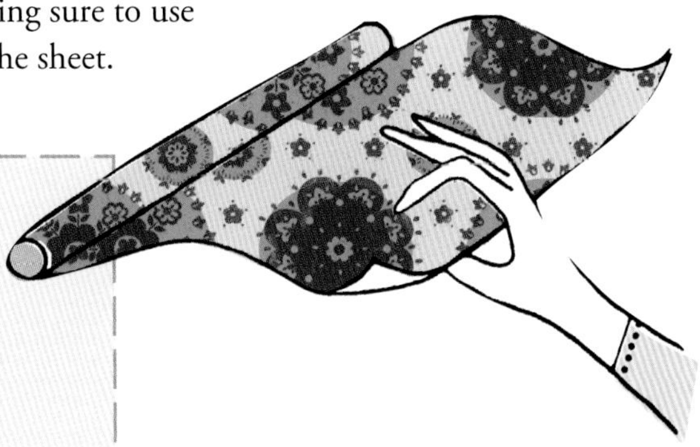

Wrapping paper
Scrapbook paper
Maps
Stamps
Paper money from
    exotic countries
Prints taken from books
Paper napkins
Tissue paper
Photographs
Postcards and
    greeting cards
Wallpaper
Stationery
Images torn from books
    or calendars
Computer-generated
    imagery
Clip art from the
    Internet
Vellum
Photocopies

Any type of paper is fair game. This list just scratches the surface.

Cutting Implements

In the project instructions, we list the most logical cutting tool as recommended by the designer, but you can substitute whichever one you're most comfortable using.

SCISSORS with sharp blades are crucial because fine cutting is so important in decoupage. Curved blades are optimal for two reasons: you can achieve smoother curves as you cut, and the blades will slightly bevel the edges of the paper, making gluing easier. However, straight-bladed embroidery scissors or manicure scissors work, too.

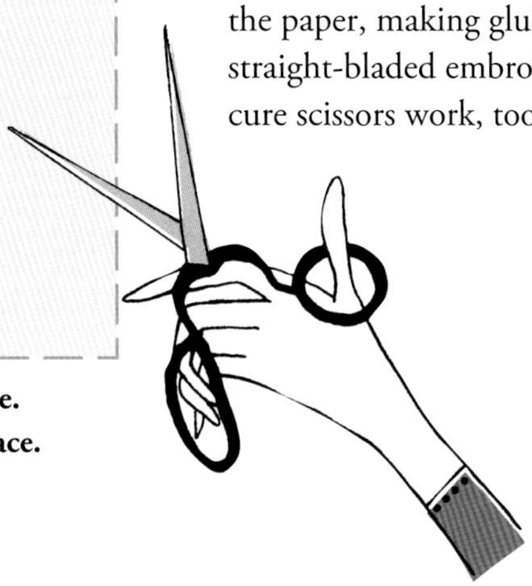

No matter which kind you use, make sure the handles feel comfortable in your fingers; the length of the scissors or of the blades doesn't matter. Reserve them only for cutting paper and never lend them out (over time, scissors conform to the hand). Carefully examine the tips with a magnifying glass—they should have perfectly sharp, matching points.

You can also buy scissors with blades that produce a decorative edge, such as deckles or scallops. They add a charming bit of detail, as shown in Baroque Picnic (see page 56). Look for these in craft stores.

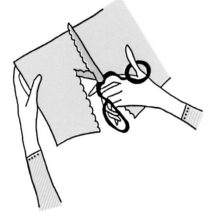

For the geeky type with deep pockets who wants a really superior cutting instrument, surgical supply companies stock stainless steel scissors that cut like a dream; find a company selling medical supplies online if your local phone book doesn't list any. Get a pair of 4½-inch (11.4 cm) curved iris scissors. (And if you're the squeamish type, don't ask what these are for.)

CRAFT KNIVES work best for cutting small, intricate areas and for cutting straight lines with a straightedge or ruler. Change the blade often so it stays sharp.

PAPER PUNCHES come in a wide variety of interesting, whimsical shapes—stars and hearts, various animals, flowers, balloons, and even silhouettes of cocktail glasses. Using them will dramatically reduce the time you spend snipping. Any craft store should carry these; look in the scrapbooking section.

PAPER CUTTERS make quick work of cutting straight lines, especially when you want them perfectly perpendicular or parallel. They cost big money, though, so you can substitute a craft knife and a straightedge.

Adhesives

Don't get stuck trying to figure out how to glue down cutouts: use the handy guide below. No matter which kind you choose, never slather it on. Using more than you need leaves behind ridges as it dries.

DECOUPAGE MEDIUM was the adhesive of choice for many of our designers because of its versatility. Use this smooth, glue-like liquid both as an adhesive and also as a protective top coat since it quickly builds up thickness. It goes on white but dries clear, and comes in two finishes: matte (some manufacturers call it satin) and gloss. All craft stores sell the stuff.

POLYVINYL ACETATE (PVA) GLUE—the plain old white household glue that you've known since childhood—works as an alternative to decoupage medium. Dilute it with water to the consistency of yogurt. PVAs are designed for porous materials only and set best at room temperature.

WALLPAPER PASTE dries more slowly than PVA glue, allowing you to mess around with the positioning of your cutout. It also gives you more time to burnish out wrinkles in the paper. It doesn't cost much, so take advantage of these qualities by adding a small amount to your primary adhesive.

WOOD GLUE can be used when attaching designs to wooden surfaces, but it's not strictly necessary.

SPRAY ADHESIVE has the advantage of drying quickly, but you'll need to know exactly where you want to place cutouts before using it. Work in a well-ventilated room, and don't forget to place a scrap of paper beneath whatever you're spraying to protect other surfaces from a sticky mess.

Protective Coatings

As mentioned earlier, decoupage medium can be used as a finish, but for a really hard, durable finish, lacquer or varnish is the way to go. As a rule of thumb, if you spray it, it's called lacquer; if you brush it on, it's varnish. Either way, it comes in various sheens, from ultra matte to high gloss. Acrylic varnish costs more, but it's a worthwhile investment because it won't yellow with age. Polyurethane clear wood varnish comes in clear and tinted shades, with high-gloss, satin, or mat finishes. You can purchase it in paint and craft stores. It's highly flammable while wet, so be careful!

MISCELLANEOUS SUPPLIES

Some projects in this book use other materials or tools than the essential ones already mentioned.

Wood Filler

It's handy to have quick-drying wood filler around in case you need to fill small holes or cracks in boxes or pieces of furniture.

Primer

Apply a coat before you paint, and you'll get better, more even color, mask uneven textures, and help your cutouts stay on. If you're starting with a dark-colored item that you want to paint a lighter shade, consider that primer is a lot cheaper than paint and will save you several coats. Look for it in spray cans.

Paints

Painting an object before gluing on cutouts beautifies it and adds a layer of visual interest. It's your call whether to take this non-essential step. Water-based paints are easier to use, but select a paint that's compatible with the material from which your object's made. For example, metal paints, available in a wide variety of colors, were developed specifically for painting on metal surfaces. Oil-based paints are more brilliant, but cost more. Thin them down with mineral spirits or paint thinner so they're easier to apply.

Latex paints, like other water-based paints, can be thinned with water. They require several coats, but dry rapidly. Acrylic paints are also water based, come in vivid colors, and dry quickly. They easily cover latex or oil-based paints. Craft stores sell them in convenient little tubes.

Abrasives

Sandpaper and steel wool smooth paint and varnishes between coats and give surfaces a bit of tooth, or roughness, onto which adhesive can stick better. Abrasives range from coarse to fine. For steel wool, the more zeros, the finer the grade. For sandpaper, the larger the number, the smoother the finish. Home improvement stores sell sanding sponges that make easy work of abrading curved surfaces.

Brushes

Our designers used both foam brushes and the conventional type; you can use either one. If you go with bristles, get the best quality you can afford, buying them from an art supply shop rather than a paint store. Cheap brushes lose stray hairs that get caught in paint, adhesive, and finishes; nothing ruins a piece of decoupage faster. Select the size of the brush according to how much surface area you need to cover. If you use water-based paints and adhesives, rinse brushes with water; otherwise, clean them with mineral spirits.

Watercolor Pencils

You'll find watercolor pencils in any store that sells fine art supplies. Use them to add color to paper cutouts or to touch up their white edges. The pigment won't run when using adhesive later, so you don't need to seal them.

Clear Spray Sealant

The inks on some papers don't remain stable after brushing on adhesive. They may discolor, run, or smear, or show bleed-through from the paper's other side. Test all your papers, and if the inks smudge, spray them with clear sealer. The section called Sealing Images (see page 16) explains how to do this. You'll find cans of this material in the paint department of home improvement stores.

Rollers

Passing a rubber roller or brayer over the glued paper immediately after positioning it removes trapped air bubbles, eliminates wrinkles, and squeezes out excess glue. Use the firm type designed for printmaking, not the spongy type for painting walls. Roll from the center out. As an alternative, you can use an expired credit card, a craft stick, a soft, clean cloth, or even your fingers if the area's small.

Wax Paper

Before passing the roller over wet, glued-down paper, place a sheet of wax paper on it to keep the tool clean. If you don't mind a gooey roller, wax paper is optional.

Photocopiers

Some of our designers saw an image in a book and didn't want to destroy it. Others scoped out great patterns on fabrics. To use those designs, they made photocopies. The decoupage work on the Versailles vanity stool (page 86), for example, originates directly from the fabric used to cover the seat. If you don't have access to a color photocopier, go to a print shop. They charge only a modest amount for copies.

Wax

Applying wax gives a mellow appearance to the decoupage. It comes in the form of either beeswax or a synthetic intended for furniture upkeep. Use wax as the final finish on decoupaged surfaces, applying it only after the varnish (or its equivalent) has completely dried. The first coat should go on thick and be left to dry for a few hours before polishing; follow it with one or two thinner layers.

TECHNIQUES

Let's be honest: decoupage isn't rocket science. You basically snip paper, stick it down on something, then add a protective coat of finish. The care you apply to cutting, gluing, and lacquering will determine how good the final product looks, but the techniques themselves are hardly complex.

Thinning the Paper

Decoupage shouldn't look like a heavy piece of paper got slapped onto an object, with a gloppy layer of finish loaded on over that. The best results come from using paper that's as light as possible. If your perfect paper is bulky, peel it to make it thinner. Before you cut out the design, dampen the back of the paper with white vinegar without soaking it. Let it sit a minute or two, then gently rub the paper with your finger or a moist sponge, rolling away layers until it's thinned. Remove the vinegar with a damp sponge and let the paper dry.

Sealing Images

Since some inks run, it's important to test a small section of your papers before cutting and gluing them. (Since you should always take this precaution, you won't get a reminder in the project instructions.) It's simple: just brush a thick coat of adhesive onto a corner of the paper. If the inks stay put, you can proceed right to snipping!

If the inks smudge, seal the paper by applying a light coat of clear spray sealer. Spray the sealant on uncut paper, allowing it to dry completely before snipping out the designs.

The wet sealant may render the paper transparent at first, but it'll dry back to opaque. If any inks interact poorly with the sealant, don't use that paper for decoupage.

Snipping Imagery

You keep being told you mastered scissors as a kid, so why include instructions on cutting? Well, this is how the pros do it. By the way, if you got scissors with curved blades, it may initially seem strange to use them, but you'll quickly get used to it.

Do your snipping near a good light source, and make sure to keep a relaxed posture. Hold the scissors however feels comfortable. The only function of the cutting hand is to open and close just the tips of the scissors. The other hand rotates the paper, guiding it between the blades.

Right-handed artists should cut clockwise in inner areas, and counterclockwise around image outlines. (If you're a southpaw, reverse these directions.) Snip out the interior sections of your design first; it's easier because there's more paper to hold. Cut in the correct direction, as explained earlier.

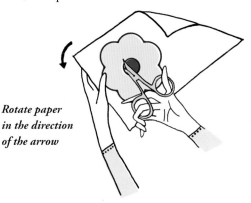

Rotate paper in the direction of the arrow

After cutting all the inner details, snip along the outside lines, working in the opposite direction.

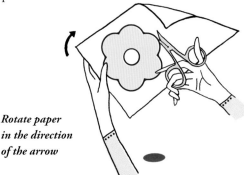

Rotate paper in the direction of the arrow

You don't need to leave bands of paper between lacy areas because even narrow paper is surprisingly strong when handled carefully. If the design tears, or you inadvertently slash off a piece of the design, no biggie: when you stick down the image later, you can glue any mistakes back into place.

Preparing Surfaces

You know how cheap apartments always look crummy because maintenance crews keep painting over top of old layers of dirty, chipped paint? Well, if you want your decoupage to look good, you've got to apply it to a smooth, clean base. The project instructions won't remind you how to prepare surfaces, so refer back to this section.

WOOD

If you want to decoupage a wooden object that's beat up or has chipped, peeling lacquer or paint, you're going to have to strip it. Pack any holes with filler, sand the entire surface smooth, and seal it with a coat of wood primer or shellac.

Give new wood a coat of primer or undercoat, or seal it with a coat of clear varnish if you want to retain the grain or color of the wood. After the wood has dried completely, sand it lightly to create a rough surface, so the paint or the adhesive you apply later will stick. For the same reason, lightly sand any varnished wood that you don't plan to paint.

Before decoupaging furniture, remove any hinges, knobs, or catches.

GLASS

Wash the piece to remove any dirt or oils, then dry it thoroughly.

METAL

If you don't remove rust on metal surfaces, it will resurface and ruin your decoupage. Buff it off with a wire brush, coarse sandpaper, or heavy-duty steel wool, then wash the surface with a solution of water and vinegar in equal proportions, and dry it thoroughly. To make sure the metal remains rust-free, prime it with two coats of rust-resistant paint. Home improvement stores sell all-in-one rust proofer and primer; follow the manufacturer's instructions.

Wash unblemished metal—including tin, enamel, and galvanized objects—with the vinegar/water solution described above or with water and detergent, then dry the object carefully. Since metal's slick, apply two coats of an oil-based primer.

CERAMIC

Make sure ceramic surfaces are free of dust before applying anything to them. Lightly sand new terra cotta, then seal it with a water-based varnish. If you decide to paint terra cotta or freshly fired bisque before gluing on cutouts, you don't need to prime it as long as the clay is clean and smooth.

Painting Surfaces

Put down at least two coats of paint to obtain good coverage. Latex paint diluted with a small quantity of water generates the ideal surface on which to decoupage. Allow each coat to dry completely, and sand it lightly before applying the next layer.

Gluing Tips

Even though you're an old hand at pasting, you probably never stopped to analyze it; this section just explains the best way to do it. Unless the instructions say otherwise, apply the adhesive to the surface of the object, not the paper: this creates less mess and prevents fragile cutouts from tearing.

Press the image down firmly with your finger, working from the center outward to push out any air bubbles. A brayer comes in handy

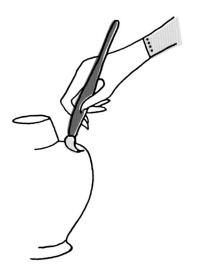

for getting rid of any remaining air bubbles, and it can also smooth paper that has inadvertently creased. If you don't have a roller, use an expired credit card, a clean cloth, or a craft stick.

If you've used PVAs or decoupage medium, wipe away any excess adhesive immediately since it dries hard fast. If you stuck the cutouts down with wallpaper paste instead, leave the piece alone for 30 minutes before wiping away the excess paste, using a cloth dampened with warm water. Waiting allows the cutouts to stick firmly and stay down despite a little rubbing.

When decoupaging onto glass, always apply the images face-down to the underside of the object. Work in reverse, gluing the foreground imagery down first, and putting the background papers on last.

Finishing Tips

You don't spend all that time and money coloring, cutting, and styling your hair without using just the right finishing product on it, right? Take the same approach in decoupage: pay the same attention to sanding, sealing, and varnishing as you do to designing, cutting, and gluing. Finishing your work protects the object as well as the decoupage, and a perfectly smooth, even surface makes the entire piece look integrated. The thinner each coat of finish, and the more coats you apply, the more refined the final appearance. A light sanding between coats enhances the overall quality of the finish.

Micromeshing is a method of polishing that uses ultra fine grades of sandpaper. This time-consuming process is well worth it for the beautiful silky glow and highly tactile surface it imparts to the work. The sanding sheets are so fine—up to 8,000 grit—that you won't find them in regular stores (by comparison, the finest grade most retailers stock is 600 grit). Businesses that specialize in woodworking and furniture restoration may sell micromesh kits, but the quickest way to find them is online. Follow the manufacturer's instructions.

DESIGN IDEAS

Cutting-edge decoupage isn't about making bad imitations of traditional decoupage. Instead, it strives to use an old technique in a fresh way. This book showcases projects that reflect the philosophy of less is more. We asked our designers to be unpredictable and to create work with a restrained, appealing aesthetic; they rose to the occasion.

Mix Styles.
Decoupeurs have always done it, so feel free to combine any images you like or find intriguing. Don't ever think you have to use an entire image; just include the interesting parts.

Choose a Focal Element.
Rather than popping a bunch of images onto an object willy-nilly, select a central motif around which to focus the rest of the pieces. For example, the Nippon Box (page 91) has an overall pattern of honeycombs surrounding the bird, which is the dominant component.

Leave Negative Space.
Blank areas spotlight the cutouts in them. Each side of the Rodeo Bins (page 78), for example, has very little on it apart from the central cutout, which allows the cowboys and girls to take a starring role.

Match Images with Objects.
Since the decoupage for Jet Set (page 52) was applied to a vintage valise, it seemed fitting to choose cutouts steeped in the style of that era. For Lunchbreak (page 29), it just made sense to put food, rather than, say, flowers, on the lunchbox. And on Baroque Picnic (page 56), the pattern on the tissue paper covering the sides of the seats complements the toile pattern atop them.

Know When to Stop.
Arrange and rearrange your cutouts before gluing them down. (If your surface is curved or vertical, reusable adhesives, like putties or waxes and low-tack, double-sided, or masking tape, will let you experiment with placement.) Try different combinations, adding and removing imagery until the composition feels right. Only then should you glue the different parts down.

Overlap Elements.
Once the design satisfies you, photograph the arrangement or make a sketch of it to note the positioning of the various elements. Then remove the cutouts and glue on the bottom elements first, adding the successive layers while referring back to your drawing or snapshot.

The Projects

Wash Day

The vintage-styled papers on these clothespins hark back to a time when people hung their laundry outside to dry.

PAPER
5 sheets of paper, each printed with a different pattern

OTHER MATERIALS
5 wooden clothespins
Decoupage medium
Fine-grit sandpaper

TOOLS
Pencil
Ruler
Craft knife
Brush or paint sponge
Scissors

tips You might use these clothespins to fasten to-do lists together or to clip opened bags of snacks closed so they remain fresh and crispy. If you glue a magnet to one face, you can place them on the refrigerator door to hang a child's drawing. Attach them upside-down to a base for displaying photographs.

WHAT YOU DO

1 Place a sheet of paper face down on the worktable. Put the flat side of a clothespin on the paper and trace around it with a pencil. Move the clothespin over an inch (2.5 cm), and trace around it a second time. Cut out both rectangles.

2 Apply a thin layer of decoupage medium to one face of the clothespin and firmly press one of the paper rectangles to it, holding the paper in place for a few seconds. Repeat on the other side of the clothespin. Trim any protruding edges with small scissors. Allow to dry.

3 Repeat steps 1 and 2 to decoupage the rest of the clothespins.

4 To give the clothespins a slightly worn appearance, lightly sand the wood alongside the edges of the paper. Apply a thin layer of decoupage medium to seal and protect your work.

DESIGNER: LuAnne Payne

Head Games

Weave these charming accessories through your tresses and you'll feel like a queen for the day. If you can't locate paper printed with the appropriate motif, hunt through a deck of cards and head for a color copier.

PAPER
Paper printed with playing cards

OTHER MATERIALS
Two natural wood checkers, each
   1¼ inches (3.2 cm) in diameter
Black acrylic paint
Decoupage medium
Fine-grit sandpaper
Two-part, quick-set epoxy
Two bobby pins
Small piece of non-drying clay
Water-based polyurethane sealant

TOOLS
Foam brushes
Pencil
Circular cutter
Self-healing cutting mat

NOTE: *Don't use an actual playing card in this project—the paper is way too stiff.*

WHAT YOU DO

1 Coat the checker pieces with black paint, allow them to dry, and apply additional coats if necessary.

2 Trace a checker twice on the paper. Using the circular cutter and working on the self-healing mat, cut out the circles.

3 Brush decoupage medium on one face of each checker as well as onto the backs of the cutout circles. Center a cutout on each checker and smooth out any wrinkles. After they've dried completely, apply an additional coat of decoupage medium to seal the paper.

4 Roughen the blank side of each checker with sandpaper, then remove the sawdust. Prepare the epoxy according to the manufacturer's instructions. Place a coin-sized amount of the adhesive in the center of each checker piece, and set the flat side of a bobby pin into each dollop of epoxy. Use clay to prop up the opposite ends of the bobby pins, so they'll remain flush with the wood as the epoxy cures overnight.

5 For additional protection from moisture and hair products, apply a coat of polyurethane sealant to the entire surface of the pieces.

tips Most craft stores sell circular cutters and self-healing mats. If you don't own these tools and don't want to make the investment, you can use a hole punch that has a 1-inch (2.5 cm) diameter. For a really low-tech approach, trace a large coin on the paper and cut out the circle, bearing in mind you won't achieve the pristine outline that you can with a specialized tool.

DESIGNER: Steven James

Clutter Cutters

These funky containers will add pizzazz to any desktop—and help keep it organized.

PAPER

Two copies each of three color laser prints of royalty-free photographs; one of scissors, one of colored pencils, and one of paper clips

OTHER MATERIALS

Three sizes of round, unfinished balsa wood containers:

5½ inches (14 cm) tall x 4¼ inches (10.8 cm) in diameter

4¾ inches (12.1 cm) tall x 3¼ inches (8.3 cm) in diameter

1⅝ inches (4.1 cm) tall x 3¾ inches (9.5 cm) in diameter

Fine sandpaper

Newspaper or paper bags

Acrylic spray paint

Gloss decoupage medium

TOOLS

Paper cutter

Foam paintbrush

WHAT YOU DO

1   If needed, gently sand the top edge of each container so it's straight and level. Clean any dust and debris off the sanded containers.

2   Spread out the newspaper or paper bags in a well-ventilated area, preferably outside. Place the containers upside down on the newspaper. Spray the surface of each container with a thin, even coat of paint. After the paint has dried completely, flip the containers right side up and lightly spray the inside of each. Allow them to dry completely.

3   Cut the images to the following dimensions. For placement on the large container, cut both scissor images to 4 x 7½ inches (10.2 x 19 cm). For the medium container, cut the two pencil images to 3½ x 7 inches (8.9 x 17.8 cm). Cut both paper clip images, which will be attached to the small container, to 1½ x 7 inches (3.8 x 17.8 cm).

DESIGNER: Marthe LeVan

4 Using the foam paintbrush, apply a thin coat of decoupage medium to the back of one trimmed image cut for the large container. Carefully adhere the image to the exterior of one side of the container, keeping the image centered and level. Apply decoupage medium to the back of the other image intended for the large container. Adhere it to the other side of the container, lining up its edges with the first image. Press out any air bubbles trapped under the paper. Immediately apply a thin coat of decoupage medium completely over the images and the exterior surface of the container, and set it aside to dry.

Repeat to adhere the images to the small- and medium-sized containers and to cover them with a coat of decoupage medium.

5 Apply additional layers of decoupage medium to achieve a more glossy appearance.

tip The balsa containers are often sold with lids, but you won't need them for this project. Pay careful attention when picking out these items at the craft store: many are misshapen. Try to select containers that have level top edges and that are as round as possible.

Lunchbreak

You'd be out to lunch to buy cafeteria food instead of packing your own meal to show off this groovy lunchbox. Although our version features traditional fare, you can choose a more exotic menu.

PAPER

4 sheets of 8½ x 11-inch (21.6 x 27.9 cm) printed paper
1 sheet of coordinating 8½ x 11-inch (21.6 x 27.9 cm) paper

OTHER MATERIALS

Metal lunchbox
Decoupage medium
Photos of lunch foods and a thermos
Clear spray sealer

TOOLS

Pencil
Ruler
Scissors
1-inch paintbrush

DESIGNER: Joan K. Morris

WHAT YOU DO

1 Cut and fit paper for the interior of the lunchbox. Put the main design in the body of the box. Place the coordinating paper inside the box lid, leaving the sides exposed. Paint decoupage medium on the backs of the pieces of paper and glue them down. Rub out any air bubbles. Brush a layer of medium over the paper and let dry.

2 Cover the outside of the lunchbox with the main paper, leaving strategic areas, such as the edges, bare. Paint decoupage medium on the back of the paper, glue it in place, and rub away air bubbles. Brush a layer of medium over the paper and let dry.

3 Cut out the food images and position them on the lunchbox in a pleasing composition. Don't forget to place some photos on the sides. Glue them in place as done in the previous steps.

4 Spray the entire box with a coat of sealer.

tips Don't feel limited to using photos of conventional lunch foods; make it a formal meal with decoupaged crystal glassware, silver utensils, and filet mignon; or go Asian with sushi, chopsticks, and saucers of artfully presented condiments. You can take digital images yourself or find clip art photos, and print them on a color printer. Try to select and arrange the cutouts so the angles at which they were taken look realistic on the box.

DESIGNER: Diana Light

Lace Vase

Turn a flea-market find into a romantic centerpiece. While the vase has a nice shape and color, it looked rather plain; the eyelet detail provides frill and contrast.

PAPER

Paper with die-cut eyelet design
Metallic paper

OTHER MATERIALS

Scrap paper
Vase
Decoupage medium

TOOLS

Pencil
Ruler
Craft knife
Circle template
Scissors
Flat brush

---

tip If you don't have a circle template, you don't need to buy one especially for this project. Simply trace around the bottom of a jar, the lip of a glass, or any other circular object you might have around that's the proper size.

WHAT YOU DO

1 Working with scrap paper, make a pattern to determine the measurements of the strip of paper to use. Make sure it fits around the curvature of the vase while still remaining flat against its entire surface. Trace the pattern onto the paper with the die-cut design, and cut it out.

2 Using the circle template, pencil a scalloped edge along one of the long back edges of the die-cut strip. Cut out the scallops.

3 Trace the scalloped strip onto the metallic paper, then cut out the design.

4 Brush decoupage medium onto the back of the metallic paper and place it on the vase, pressing down and smoothing out any air bubbles with your fingers. Allow the medium to dry completely.

5 Brush decoupage medium onto the metallic paper and press the die-cut paper in place over it. Smooth out any air bubbles. Let the medium dry.

6 Brush decoupage medium on the die-cut paper and apply some to the vase just a minimal distance around the paper's edge. Allow the medium to dry.

Fanfare

Vintage-style fans already look cool, and applying paper in warm tones of blue, green, and orange ratchets up the hipness quotient still more.

PAPER
5 sheets of patterned paper from a 6-inch (15.2 cm) square scrapbooking pad

OTHER MATERIALS
Table fan
Adhesive designed specifically for bonding materials to metal
Acrylic gloss medium

TOOLS
Scrap cardstock
Pencil
Scissors or craft knife
1-inch foam brush

tip Since the fan blades are curved, heavyweight papers won't bend and adhere to them as easily as lighter ones. Cut the stencil slightly bigger all the way around to leave enough allowance for the curvature; otherwise, you may not have enough paper to cover the entire blade. You'll trim away any excess paper from the blade edges after gluing it on the blade.

NOTE: *This project is for decorative use only.*

WHAT YOU DO

1 Remove the grille and blades from the fan. Trace one of the fan blades onto the scrap cardstock. Cut out the shape to create a stencil for the blades (see the Tip).

2 Using a different pattern of paper each time, trace the stencil onto as many sheets as the fan has blades. Cut the shapes out.

3 Use the adhesive to attach each paper cutout to the top of a fan blade. Allow it to dry completely. Afterward, use either small detail scissors or a craft knife to trim off any excess paper along the blade edges, then coat the top of each fan blade with acrylic gloss medium.

4 Cut out a circle of the right size to attach to the center of the grille. Position it, and glue it down. After the glue dries completely, seal the paper with acrylic gloss medium.

5 Reassemble the fan.

DESIGNER:
Nicole Novak Luperini

DESIGNER: Terry Taylor

Confetti

Let the kids join in on this project!
All you need is colorful wrapping
paper and a few paper punches...
along with the willingness to
surrender creative control.

PAPER

Colorful, striped wrapping paper

OTHER MATERIALS

2 child-sized wooden chairs
Sandpaper
Acrylic paint in two shades
Decoupage medium
Acrylic varnish

TOOLS

Brushes
Ruler
Craft knife
Decorative paper punches

tip   While this project features
paper dots in three different sizes, you
can find punches that create a variety of
more exotic motifs—hearts, locomotives,
leaves, and dogs, among others—in the
scrapbooking section of craft retailers.

WHAT YOU DO

1 If your chairs are finished, sand them
before painting them. If you're using
unfinished chairs, simply paint them as desired.
(To avoid a lot of cleanup, you might not ask
the kids to help with this task.) Allow the paint
to dry.

2 Cut the paper into strips the width of
your paper punches. Round up your help-
ers and have them punch out plenty of shapes.
They may say they've punched out a bunch,
but assure them you can never have too many.

3 Have the kids adhere the punch-outs to
the chairs using decoupage medium.
(They'll undoubtedly tire of the novelty quickly,
so be prepared to finish the project yourself!)
Allow everything to dry.

4 Give the chairs one or more coats of
varnish to protect the paper.

Creative Blocks

Set on a desk, shelf, or mantel, these cubes add some retro flair. The simplicity of the design belies their decorating potential—the blocks can be arranged in a variety of playful combinations.

PAPER

16 small sheets of paper, each printed with a different pattern

OTHER MATERIALS

3 small wooden blocks, each 1¼ inches (3.2 cm) square

1 large wooden block, 3½ inches (8.9 cm) square

Decoupage medium

TOOLS

Pencil

Ruler

Craft knife

Brush or paint sponge

Scissors

Fine-grit sandpaper (optional)

tips

Because each plane of the cubes is so small, you don't need large sheets for this project, but can use the leftover scraps of your favorite papers that you've carefully saved just in case a special project came along. Although the designer usually chooses a different pattern for each side, she sometimes likes to cover an entire block with the same paper.

WHAT YOU DO

1 Place a small block on a piece of paper, lining up one corner with one of the corners of the sheet. Lightly trace around the block with a pencil. Repeat with other pieces of paper to trace five more squares.

2 Cut around each traced square.

3 Apply a thin layer of decoupage medium to one side of the block. Press a paper square firmly onto the block, holding it in place for a few seconds. If the square is a bit too large, carefully trim it with small scissors. Remove any excess glue with a damp paper towel. Repeat, covering all sides of the block. Allow to dry.

4 Repeat steps 1 to 3 on the remaining blocks, including the large one.

5 To give the blocks a vintage appearance, lightly sand the edges and corners with fine-grit sandpaper. Cover each side with another thin layer of decoupage medium to protect your work.

Light Waves

These plain, frosted lamps, embellished with brightly colored translucent tissue paper, cast a groovy glow in even the squarest room. Follow the paper's printed patterns or cut out shapes of tissue that appeal to your sense of design.

PAPER
Patterned tissue paper

OTHER MATERIALS
3 frosted glass lamps
Decoupage medium

TOOLS
Scissors
Flat brush

tip You're not limited to horizontal stripes, but could instead opt for vertical ones, diagonals, or even crisscrossed strips. The sky's the limit.

WHAT YOU DO

1 Cut strips of patterned paper, following the pattern design or creating one of your own.

2 Carefully wrap one strip of tissue around the circumference of a lamp. Cut the strip to fit, allowing a tiny bit for an overlap. If needed, trim the width of the ends of the strip to create a seamless join. Apply decoupage medium to the lamp just where you intend to adhere the strip, and place the strip down on it. Take care not to tear the tissue as you smooth it down on the surface. Before it dries, clean the excess medium from the lamp surface with a damp paper towel.

3 Add strips to each of the lamps. Vary the number of strips and their widths to give the grouping a lively sense of design.

4 Give the applied strips a coating of medium to protect the paper.

DESIGNER: Terry Taylor

Quotable Cabinet

Add a little humor to the most serious of places. This filing cabinet will help you keep things in perspective, even through a long day of work.

DESIGNER: Wendi Gratz

MATERIALS

Filing cabinet
Sandpaper
Masking tape
Metal primer
Paint
Glue
Polyurethane

TOOLS

Large brush
Measuring tape
Computer and
  color printer
Craft knife
Small brush
Tweezers

WHAT YOU DO

1 Lightly sand the entire cabinet, and mask off the handles and keyhole. Prime it, allow it to dry completely, then paint it.

2 Determine how you want to wrap the quote around the cabinet, and measure the distance it will cover.

Choose a quote and type it up in a word-processing document. Select a color and a font for the text—choose one that isn't narrow, to make it easier to cut and glue. Next comes the tricky part: adjust the point size of the font, experimenting until the sum of the length of each line equals the entire length you want to cover.

3 Print the document and confirm that the text fills up exactly the space it should. Do so by cutting roughly around the words and arranging them on the filing cabinet in their intended location. Adjust the font size as necessary, printing and checking until the fit is right. Once it is, use a craft knife to cut out the letters precisely.

4 Use glue mixed with a little water to bond the letters to the cabinet. (It may help to use tweezers to guide them into position.) To fold a letter over a corner, let the glue soften the paper a bit, then coax it over the bend with the brush. Letters split by the gap between the drawer and the plane of the file cabinet should be cut before gluing them on, since the paper will more likely tear than slice cleanly when wet. Let the glue dry overnight, then brush over each letter with more watered-down glue.

5 Apply up to 20 coats of polyurethane. Paint on many thin coats instead of a few thick ones to prevent the finish from looking cloudy. Between each coat, sand lightly with 220-grit sandpaper, then thoroughly wipe away any dust.

tips You can use the same quote as our designer did, or find your own. Any library should contain books of quotations, indexed by subject matter. You can also easily find websites listing citations on practically any topic by typing "quotations" in your favorite search engine.

Hanging in Style

There's a certain type of woman who can never have too many shoes or handbags. This project celebrates her existence. Of course, draping anything but scarves or pants on these hangers will hide the designs.

PAPER
Napkins printed with purses and shoes

MATERIALS
Sandwich bag
2 wooden clothes hangers
Fine-grit sandpaper or 320-grit sanding sponge
Decoupage medium

TOOLS
Scissors
Brush

tip Clamping the hangers in a table vise during the process of applying the cutouts freed up both hands to handle the delicate napkin paper.

WHAT YOU DO

1 Cut out images of the pumps and purses, avoiding the ones printed on the textured edges. Gently separate the layers of napkin, keeping only the printed sheet. Store them in a sandwich bag because the slightest waft will cause them to flutter away.

2 Lightly sand the hangers.

3 Paint a very thin coat of decoupage medium to the hangers on the areas where you'd like to attach the handbag and shoe images. Place the images on the medium and lightly press down on them with your fingers. Allow them to dry.

4 Paint three coats of decoupage medium all over the hangers, allowing it to dry between applications.

DESIGNER: Nathalie Mornu

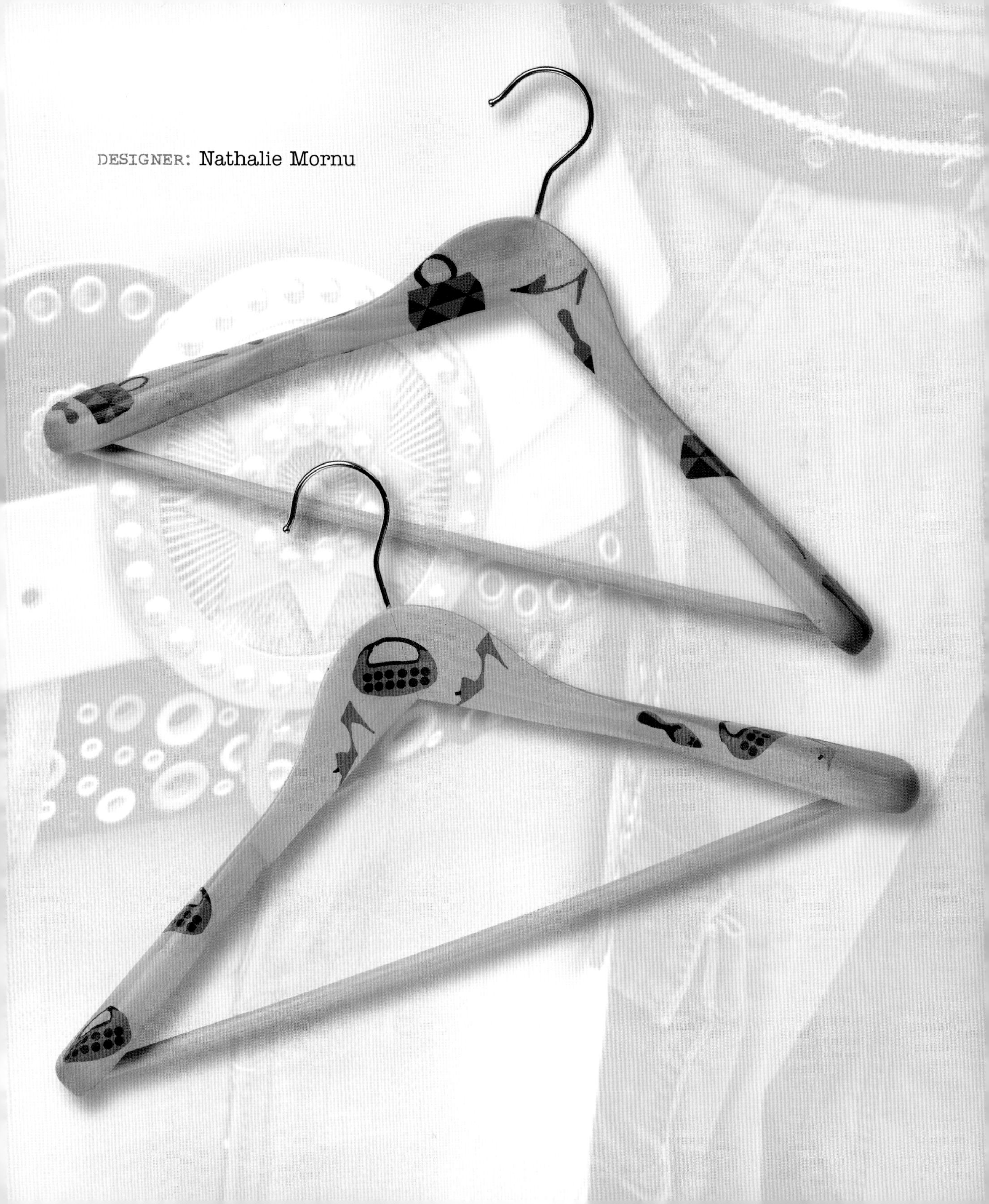

Eggs-Ceptional

What is it about eggs that invites puns? A mosaic of colorful origami paper, applied methodically, evokes tiles on a roof or scales on a pinecone.

DESIGNER: Steven James

PAPER

2 sheets of patterned origami paper
  per egg, each 4½ inches (11.4 cm)
  square

OTHER MATERIALS

3 small wooden eggs
White acrylic paint
Decoupage medium

TOOLS

Foam brush
Paper punch with a diameter of
  ½ inch (1.3 cm) or less (see
  the Tips)
Small craft brush

tips Smaller paper circles will lie flatter on curved surfaces, which are more prominent at the ends of the eggs. To create very small cutouts, consider using a standard office hole punch, which produces the ideal size of circle for this project. If you don't already own one at home, maybe you can avoid buying this tool by borrowing one overnight from work. Don't forget to return it!

WHAT YOU DO

1 Paint the surface of each egg with the white acrylic paint, using the foam brush. (This will brighten its appearance.) Allow the paint to dry, brushing on additional coats as necessary.

2 Use the paper punch to cut out circles from the paper. Punch out every sheet, aiming to cut as many circles as possible from each.

3 Using the craft brush, apply decoupage medium onto the back of a cutout. Adhere it to the center of the egg. Smooth down the paper, then apply an additional coat of medium over it. Remove any excess adhesive.

Working around the narrow circumference of the egg, attach consecutive cutouts, each slightly over the edge of the previous one. Clean the craft brush frequently to remove any superfluous medium that glops up the bristles of the brush. Thoroughly dry the brush to remove excess water, and resume the process.

Apply consecutive rows from the center to either tip of the egg until you've completely covered it. To ensure a smooth surface, finger press the cutouts at the ends of the egg, since the curves are more significant in these areas.

4 Repeat step 3 on the remaining eggs.

5 Using the foam brush, apply a final sealer coat of decoupage medium to the surface of each egg, and allow it to dry.

Seashore

Decoupage was all the rage during the Rococo era, when shells were a popular motif in the decorative arts. A simple touch—just the image of a whorled conch—is all you need to create an elegant piece of jewelry.

PAPER
Line drawing of shells

OTHER MATERIALS
Mother-of-pearl pendant
Decoupage medium
Clear gloss acrylic spray varnish
1 large silver jump ring
1 yard (0.9 m) of silk cord
Beading thread
12 flat-bottomed 5-mm pearls
12 seed beads

TOOLS
Craft knife
Fine-tipped brush
2 sets of pliers
Beading needle

tips Our designer found the illustration while thumbing through a vintage dictionary. He didn't mind cutting up the book, but you may not feel that way. If necessary, simply photocopy the drawing you wish to use. Look for mother-of-pearl pendants in stores or catalogs that stock jewelry-making supplies.

WHAT YOU DO

1 Carefully cut out the image. Apply it to the pendant using decoupage medium. Allow the medium to dry.

2 Spray the pendant with acrylic varnish.

3 Use the jump ring to hang the pendant on the cord. Don't pull the ends of the jump ring straight apart, laterally, since this will distort its shape. The correct way to open and close jump rings is to hold each end with pliers; twist one end toward you and the other end away, as shown in figure 1.

4 Thread a beading needle with thread. Stitch the pearls—each topped by a seed bead to accentuate it—to the midpoint of the cord, placing them on either side in a cluster that holds the jump ring and pendant in position. Finish each end of the cord with a small, tight knot, and tie the cord to wear it.

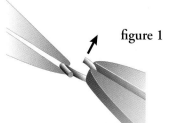

figure 1

DESIGNER: Terry Taylor

Doily

This delicate side table called out for a lacy covering, but one with a contemporary twist. The designs gain a unique visual texture from the paper's motif—a subtle floral printed in copper ink.

PAPER
1 large sheet of patterned paper

OTHER MATERIALS
Three-legged wooden table
Sandpaper
Acrylic spray paint
Template of your choice
Decoupage medium
Acrylic varnish

TOOLS
Photocopier
Scissors
Stapler
Spiral paper punch
Craft knife
Flat brush

WHAT YOU DO

1 Lightly sand the entire table to abrade its surface, then give it several coats of acrylic spray paint.

2 Use a photocopier to reduce or enlarge your template as desired, then make enough copies of it to arrange on the table to determine fit and how many motifs to cut. (This will save you the tedium of cutting out far more pieces than you need.)

3 Trim each photocopy near the outline of the design and attach each to the patterned paper by stapling around the exterior of the line. Be excessive with the staples, as they'll keep the paper from shifting during the cutting process. Cut out the shapes, removing the inner portions first, then working your way outward to the exterior lines.

Use the paper punch to create small spirals. Glue these to the table, varying their orientation for visual interest.

4 Place the cutout motifs on the table. Play with their composition, varying the orientation of the spirals to add visual interest; what you originally had in mind might change once you start arranging the shapes.

5 Using decoupage medium, adhere one shape at a time to the table. Make sure all of the edges are stuck down before applying the next shape. After all the motifs are attached, allow them to dry.

6 Give the tabletop several coats of acrylic varnish to protect the paper.

tip Any number of sources exist for finding a template for the tabletop: you can purchase commercial stencils from a craft store, enlarge a line drawing taken from a book of designs, search for botanical motifs online, borrow and alter a portion of a larger pattern, or simply doodle your own.

DESIGNER: Terry Taylor

DESIGNER: Joan K. Morris

Jet Set

This valise evokes the glamour of an era when people dressed up to travel. Scour secondhand stores to find a similar suitcase.

MATERIALS

Round vintage suitcase

Illustration of a cityscape

Decoupage medium

Vintage photo of a fashion model or flight attendant

Clear gloss spray sealer

TOOLS

Color photocopier

Scissors

Paintbrush

> **tip** Look for interesting illustrations in unexpected places. When our designer needed a cityscape, she happened to be in a fabric store and spotted just what she needed on a bolt of material. If you can't locate a vintage magazine photo of a flight attendant, you might have better luck finding one online on a clip art website.

WHAT YOU DO

1 Make enough photocopies of the cityscape to cover the lower portion of both the front and the back of the suitcase, as well as the bottoms of its sides.

2 Cut out the shapes of the buildings that will create the skyline of the city. Cut out other buildings to fill in the foreground, if necessary.

3 Paint decoupage medium onto the suitcase in the area to cover. Working in sections, place cutouts in the medium and rub out any bubbles or wrinkles. Matching up the lines, glue the next section in place. Repeat until the front, back and sides are covered.

4 On the photocopier, enlarge or reduce the photo of the model or flight attendant to fit the design. Glue the image into place. Allow all of the adhesive to dry completely.

5 Following the manufacturer's instructions, spray two coats of clear sealer spray. (Use more coats if you plan on using the suitcase where it will be exposed to damp weather.)

Fish Hooks

Deciding the type of image to decoupage onto these wall hooks was a no-brainer: the hooks immediately brought to mind the words "fish hook," which presented a ready opportunity for some visual punning.

PAPER
Coordinating wrapping paper in three colorways
Seven images of fish

OTHER MATERIALS
5 block-shaped wall hooks
Decoupage medium

TOOLS
Paper cutter
Brush
Brayer
Scissors

tip Look for copyright-free digital images of two different fish on the Internet, then use a graphic-design program to resize them, apply different colors to the original black line work, and flip them to face in different directions.

WHAT YOU DO

1 Cut out squares and rectangles of various sizes from the wrapping paper. You'll apply these to the wooden part of the hooks, and can opt for more or less coverage of the block.

2 Using decoupage medium, apply the squares and rectangles to the blocks, placing them in pleasing arrangements on all the visible faces. Use a brayer to get all the air bubbles out and make certain the edges bond down perfectly flush.

3 Cut out the fish. Determine where to place them, then glue them down with decoupage medium.

4 To seal your work, apply three coats of decoupage medium to the entire surface, allowing each to dry between applications.

DESIGNER: Nathalie Mornu

Baroque Picnic

The pastoral pattern on the wrapping paper was inspired by an antique toile wallpaper in the collection of a museum. The scalloped edge on the spinning seats adds a fancy touch.

PAPER
2 sheets of patterned tissue paper
2 sheets of wrapping paper printed with a toile pattern

OTHER MATERIALS
Wooden bench with three seats
Scrap paper
Decoupage medium
Varnish

TOOLS
Pencil
Ruler or tape measure
Scissors
Stapler
Scalloped-edge scissors
Flat brush

WHAT YOU DO

1 Remove the seats. Measure the height and circumference of one. Mark and cut a strip of tissue slightly longer than the circumference and 1½ inches (3.8 cm) wider than the height. Repeat for the other seats.

2 Place a seat upside down on a piece of scrap paper, and create a template by tracing around it. Make as many templates as there are seats on the bench. Roughly cut out each template, leaving about ¼ inch (6 mm) around the outline.

3 Staple each template to the patterned paper around the outer edge of the template. Cut along the outlines using the scalloped-edge scissors.

4 Adhere the tissue strips to the sides of the seats with decoupage medium, centering them so the excess paper extends evenly beyond either edge. Once the sides are smoothly covered, make small vertical cuts in the excess tissue, and fold it over the top and bottom of the seat. Allow it to dry.

5 Center the patterned paper on the seat tops and adhere each with decoupage medium. Allow them to dry.

6 Give the covered surfaces several coats of varnish or decoupage medium to protect the paper.

DESIGNER: Terry Taylor

DESIGNER: Diana Light

Play Time

This striking set of clocks would fit perfectly on a nursery wall or schoolroom. Besides being fun to make, they might prompt discussions about geography, time zones, and old-fashioned toys.

PAPER
World map
Striped vellum
Wrapping paper printed with toys

OTHER MATERIALS
4 clocks
Gloss decoupage medium
Clear spray sealer

TOOLS
Pencil
Craft knife
Flat brush
Wax paper
Brayer

NOTE: *Repeat steps 1 through 6 for each clock.*

WHAT YOU DO

1 Remove the hand mechanism from one of the clocks. Place the clock face down on the map, trace around its circumference, and cut the circle out of the paper. Brush decoupage medium on the clock face and place the circle cut from the map on it, carefully lining up the edges. Place the wax paper over the map, then use the brayer to smooth away any air bubbles. Pull off the wax paper and let the decoupage medium dry.

2 Trace the clock face on the striped vellum, and cut out the circle. Draw a cross through its middle, dividing it into identical quarters and keeping the lines parallel to, or perpendicular to, the stripes in the paper, as the case may be. Cut out the quarters. Use decoupage medium to attach one quarter to any quadrant of the clock; attach a second quarter to the opposite quadrant. As in step 1, place wax paper over the vellum and use the brayer to smooth away air pockets, then allow the medium to dry. The vellum paper will bubble up, but if it's left alone, it will flatten back out as it dries.

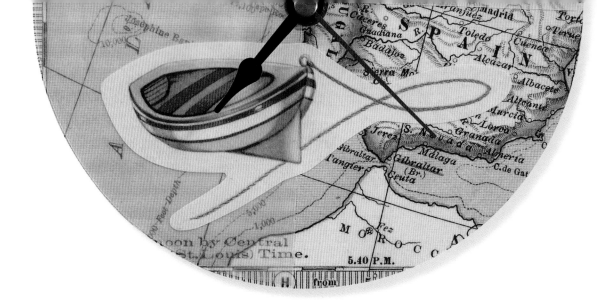

3 Carefully cut out the center hole through which you'll later replace the clockworks. Use the knife to trim any excess paper from the edges of the clock face.

4 Cut out a drawing of a toy, keeping the cut about ¼ inch (6 mm) from the edge of the drawing. Attach the image to the clock in the way described in step 1. Brush decoupage medium onto the edges of the clock, too. Let it dry.

5 Coat the entire project with clear spray paint. Allow it to dry completely.

6 Replace the hands on the clock.

Corinthian Shade

The elegant print of this shade is both sophisticated and playful. The symmetrical arrangement of the pattern conjures images of Roman columns.

PAPER

2 large sheets of patterned
  wrapping paper

OTHER MATERIALS

Ceramic lamp with a drum shade
Quick-drying adhesive spray
  designed specifically for paper
White spray primer
Spray paint

TOOLS

Tape measure
Pencil
Ruler
Craft knife
Scissors
Clothespins or paper clips

WHAT YOU DO

1 Measure the height and circumference of the shade. Add 2 inches (5.1 cm) to the circumference measurement for the seam overlap, and 2 inches (5.1 cm) to the height. Draw a rectangle of these dimensions on the back of the paper, and cut it out.

2 Turn the top edge of the rectangle under 1 inch (2.5 cm). Do the same on the bottom edge.

DESIGNER: Colette George

3 To add more layers of visual interest, cut out sections of the remaining paper to decoupage onto the rectangle. Spray a very thin layer of adhesive onto the backs of the cutouts and glue them into place.

4 Wrap the paper around the shade. Use adhesive spray to affix it to the shade in a few discreet places, as well as along the entire seam of the overlapping edges. Hold the paper in place with clothespins or paper clips until it dries.

5 Spray the lamp base with white primer. After it has dried completely, spray the base in a color that coordinates with the patterned paper.

variation

You can apply patterned paper directly to smooth shades, but some lamp shades have an uneven surface texture that requires you to cover them with a stiff paper, such as wallpaper liner, to which you can mount the patterned paper.

In this case, cut the liner paper to the dimensions as instructed in step 1, and for the patterned paper, add 4 inches (10.2 cm) to the circumference as well as to the height. Place the patterned paper face-down and center the liner paper over it. Mark the placement of the liner paper, remove it, and use adhesive spray to adhere it to the patterned paper. Fold the top and bottom allowances of the patterned paper over the edges of the liner paper, creasing them neatly with a fingertip to avoid ripping the paper or having any of its color lift away.

Proceed from step 3; for step 4, center the covered liner along the height of the lamp shade.

Vivid Vitrine

The metallic background of the paper lends a golden glow to this cabinet. The spacing of the paper squares was designed to obscure more of the interior in some places, less in others. In the right light, the decoupage casts a lovely shadow.

PAPER

Wrapping paper printed with
  colorful squares on a gold
  background

OTHER MATERIALS

Cabinet with a glass door
Decoupage medium
Brayer and wax paper (optional)
Cotton swabs

TOOLS

Ruler or straightedge
Pencil
Paper cutter, scissors, or craft knife
½-inch (1.3 cm) flat brush

WHAT YOU DO

1 Remove the door from the cabinet and place it on the work surface; it's much easier to arrange and attach the paper cutouts if you're working on a horizontal plane.

2 Decide how many rows you wish to have on the door, as well as the number of paper squares you want in each row. Multiply these two numbers, and cut out that amount of squares, making them all the same size. (Our designer opted for 34 rows; she decided to alternate areas with denser rows of five squares each, and more open areas that alternate between having either two or three squares in them.)

3 Arrange the squares on the *front* of the glass in the pattern you want. If you wish, you can move the squares around to improvise a different placement than you had originally planned.

DESIGNER: Diana Light

4 Lift up a square, brush decoupage medium onto the glass where it was laid, replace the square, and use your fingers or a piece of wax paper and a brayer to smooth it down. Use a cotton swab moistened with water to wipe off any excess decoupage medium.

Repeat to glue down each square. Let the piece dry completely.

5 Go back over the edge of each square with decoupage medium, brushing only a minimal amount of medium on the glass. Allow to dry.

6 Mount the door back onto the shelf. The designer also opted to change the original plain wooden doorknob to something with a little more pizzazz.

tip If you wish to keep the grid perfectly square, you can make a guide to follow. Cut a piece of butcher paper to the exact dimensions of the glass panel. With the help of vertical and horizontal rules, measure and mark the exact placement of all the squares on it. Tape this piece of paper to the back of the glass, place the square cutouts on the front of the glass exactly atop the placement marks, and mount them with medium.

Mirrors, Mirrors, on the Wall

The flowers may look painted on, but that's just smoke and mirrors—they're really cut from paper. The trick is simply to select a paper printed in a motif with a dabbed appearance.

PAPER
3 sheets of wrapping paper printed
  with flowers

OTHER MATERIALS
9 mirrors framed in unfinished
  wood
Primer
Acrylic or latex paint
Decoupage medium
Wax paper

TOOLS
Masking tape
Flat brush
Measuring tape
Scissors
Small brush
Brayer

WHAT YOU DO

1   To protect it from spattered paint, apply masking tape over the mirror glass. Apply primer to the frames and let it dry. Paint the frames and allow them to dry.

   Determine how you plan to hang the frames on the wall—including the distances separating them—and place them exactly in that way on a work surface.

DESIGNER: Diana Light

2 Cut the flowers out of the paper. Arrange them on, around, and between the frames, trying various combinations until you've achieved a pleasing composition. (To help you remember the placement of the cutouts later, make a quick sketch or take a digital photo.)

3 Using a small quantity of decoupage medium, affix the flowers arranged on the fronts of the frames to the wood. If the cutouts extend over the front plane of the frame, bend them around the corner; if, after doing so, they extend past the back edge of the side, cleanly trim them off along that edge, and glue them down. Save any trimmed-off pieces to attach to the wall later, making note of their eventual placement.

Place wax paper over the frames and roll the brayer over them to smooth out any air bubbles. After the frames dry, brush on two more coats of medium, allowing them to dry in between.

Once they've dried, remove the tape from the mirror glass.

4 Hang the frames on the wall. Referring to the sketch or photo made earlier, use decoupage medium to stick the remaining flowers, as well as the bits trimmed off in step 3, to the wall. Apply the decoupage medium only on the paper, not on the wall.

5 After the medium dries, apply two more coats, allowing them to dry between applications. Make sure to brush as little decoupage medium as possible past the outlines of the cutouts and onto the wall.

> **tip** Painting the wall in a color identical to the background color of the paper will enhance the illusion that the design has been brushed on with pigment. Mask the presence of the decoupage medium by using a type with the same finish—glossy or matte—as that of the paint.

All Aflutter

These decorative tiles fit perfectly over the burners of a gas stove, brightening the kitchen. With four of them to make, there's plenty of opportunity to experiment with various layouts of the design elements.

PAPER

4 sheets of paper printed with a wallpaper motif, for the background

3 sheets of cardstock in a color contrasting with the background paper, for the stripes

2 sheets of paper with a textured, denim-like finish, for the butterflies

OTHER MATERIALS

4 ceramic tiles, each 8 inches (20.3 cm) square

Glue

2 fine-tipped permanent markers, in colors matching the cardstock and the textured paper

Scrap cardstock

Acrylic gloss medium

16 rubber feet or chair tips (available at home improvement stores)

TOOLS

Metal ruler

Craft knife

1-inch foam brush

Photocopier

Pencil

Hot glue gun

WHAT YOU DO

1 Cut four pieces of background paper to the size of the ceramic tiles. Use glue to attach these to the tops of the tiles. Allow them to dry.

2 Using a marker that's the same color as the non-textured cardstock, fill in selected areas of the paper's motifs.

3 Cut out strips of varying widths from the non-textured cardstock. After determining a satisfying arrangement, attach them to the background paper using glue.

4 Photocopy the butterfly-shaped templates on page 96. Cut out the templates, trace their outlines onto scrap cardstock, and cut those out to create stencils. Trace the stencils onto the denim-textured cardstock—for this project, our designer used five big ones and three small—and cut them out. After positioning them in a pleasing composition, glue the butterfly silhouettes to the tile faces.

5 Color the edges of the tiles with a permanent marker of the same color as the butterfly cut-outs. Seal the entire top of the tile with several coats of acrylic gloss medium, brushing it on thinly and allowing it to dry in between applications.

6 Attach the chair tips or rubber feet to each corner of the tiles using hot glue.

tip To turn these into functional trivets, simply have ¼-inch-thick pieces of glass cut to fit the tops of the tiles. Ask for a type resistant to thermal shock, and attach the panes over the decoupage work with clear epoxy.

DESIGNER: Nicole Novak Luperini

Coleoptera Platter

Natural beauty adorns this dish. Working on the underside of the glass makes the platter look seamless, creating an elegant impression.

PAPER

Striped paper

Paper printed with old-fashioned
  script for the background

OTHER MATERIALS

Image of an insect

5 insect-related words (see the Tip
  on page 000)

Glass plate, 5½ x 11¾ inches
  (14 x 29.8 cm)

Matte medium

Water-based varnish

Gold-colored permanent marker

TOOLS

Scissors

2 medium-sized brushes

Craft knife

Paint scraper

NOTE: *When decoupaging onto glass, always attach the images face-down to the underside of the object unless instructed otherwise.*

WHAT YOU DO

1 Cut out the insect and the words. Cut four strips of the striped paper, each 5⁄16 inch (8 mm) wide and the length of the plate's sides.

2 Turn the plate upside down, eyeball where you wish to place the insect image, and paint matte medium onto that area. (It bears repeating: be sure to attach the paper face-down on the underside of the object.) Place the image on the matte medium. Working from the center of the image outward, press out any air bubbles and extra adhesive.

3 Determine where to place the words along the plate edges, paint matte medium onto those spots, and use the method described in step 2 to attach them. Allow them to dry, then attach the striped strips with more matte medium along all the edges, gluing them directly over the words. Allow the medium to dry.

DESIGNER: Judy Carmichael

4 Brush matte medium over the entire bottom of the plate and glue the background paper to it (see the Tip). Trim away any extra paper with a craft knife, and allow the plate to dry.

5 Apply four coats of varnish to the bottom of the plate. After the varnish dries, pick up just a wee bit of paint on the tip of a dry brush. Lightly graze the bottom of the plate with the brush to give it an antiqued appearance.

6 Use a paint scraper to remove dried matte medium and varnish from the plate's edge. Draw a line of gold along the edge of the plate with the marking pen.

tip To make it easier to fit the background paper over the plate's curves, the designer cut the background paper into horizontal strips. She applied a watercolor wash to each; it emphasizes the aged look of the paper, and also disguises the seams between the seven strips she used.

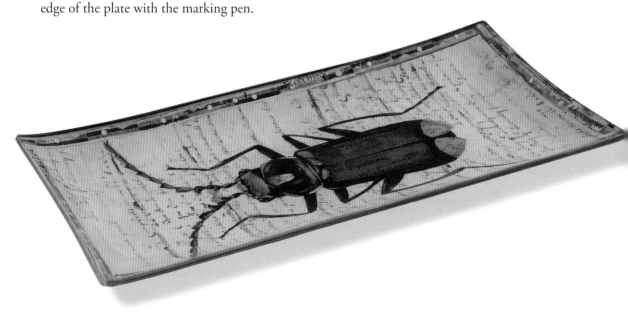

Primavera

An unusual bleaching technique used on vellum makes this leafy design look like it's been painted with watercolors.

PAPER
20 sheets of chartreuse vellum, each 8 ½ x 11 inches (21.6 x 27.9 cm)

OTHER MATERIALS
4 or 5 fern fronds
Newspaper
Bleach
Wooden chair with cutout back
White paint or primer
Decoupage medium
Gloss spray sealer

TOOLS
1-inch brush
Scissors
Old credit card
Craft knife

WHAT YOU DO

1 Work in a well-ventilated area while bleaching the vellum. Begin by putting a fern frond right-side up on a piece of newspaper. Brush bleach on the leaves and the center stem, then carefully place the fern on the vellum with the bleach facing down. Hold the frond in place with one finger, and press the leaf and the stem onto the vellum. The bleach will begin to lighten the vellum immediately.

Remove the leaf, putting it back on the newspaper right-side up. Reapply bleach on it and bleach more designs onto all of the vellum sheets (each sheet may hold several bleached designs). Allow them to dry.

DESIGNER: Joan K. Morris

2 Remove the seat from the chair. Paint the chair white, and let it dry.

3 Cut rectangular pieces of various sizes out of the vellum. Each should contain a bleached design with some space around it.

4 Work section by section to apply the vellum rectangles to the chair. Brush decoupage medium onto the back of a piece of vellum, as well as onto a small area of the chair. Place the paper on the chair, orienting the design vertically—don't attach the paper at an angle—and sweep a credit card across it, working from the center outward, to remove bubbles and wrinkles. Removing all of the wrinkles takes effort, but as the vellum dries, it will shrink and flatten out more.

5 Repeat step 4 to cover the entire chair, overlapping the edges of the rectangles and wrapping them around corners where necessary. Apply vellum to the entire chair apron, so as not to leave any visually jarring blank spots when you reattach the seat later.

6 After allowing the decoupage medium to dry overnight, spray a coat of gloss sealer over the whole chair. Let it dry, then reattach the seat.

tips You can purchase fern fronds from a florist. Begin applying the pieces of cut-up vellum to the back of the chair, where they'll be less visible while you get the hang of the technique. If your chair has openwork in the back like the one pictured here, glue a vellum rectangle to cover an entire opening and use a craft knife to cut an X from corner to corner. Fold the resulting flaps in toward the center, and glue them down. As you work, check for small spots left uncovered, and glue small pieces of vellum over them.

Rodeo Bins

When they're all done horsin' around, the kids can round up their toys and keep 'em corralled in these old-fashioned toy boxes.

PAPER

Clip art or photo of rope

OTHER MATERIALS

2 wooden boxes, each 15 inches (38.1 cm) square and 12 inches (30.5 cm) tall, with casters
Paint
Fabric printed with cowboys and cowgirls
Decoupage medium
Clear gloss spray sealer

TOOLS

2-inch paintbrush
Color photocopier
Scissors
1-inch brush

WHAT YOU DO

1 Remove the casters. Paint the boxes and let them dry.

2 On a color copier, copy cowboy and cowgirl designs from the fabric, enlarging or reducing them to fit the box panels. Copy eight images—one for each side of each box. Cut out the designs, carefully snipping the details.

3 Apply decoupage medium onto a box in the area where you wish to place a paper design. Place the cutout onto the medium, paint over it with additional medium to seal it, and rub away any bubbles or wrinkles. Repeat, placing the cutouts on all four sides of both boxes. Let the medium dry for an hour.

4 Assemble enough of the rope image to edge all four sides of each panel. Cut out the rope.

5 Working in sections, paint decoupage medium around all four sides of each panel, about ¼ inch (6 mm) from the edges, then adhere the rope images to it. Paint over all the rope designs with medium. Allow it to dry.

6 Following the manufacturer's instructions, apply two or three coats of clear spray sealer. After the last coat has dried, reattach the casters.

tips You'll find large selections of cloth printed with playful designs in the children's department of specialty fabric retailers, as well as in stores that specialize in quilting. To make the rope look more realistic, orient it with the shadows facing in the same direction. As you add pieces, match the ends of the rope.

DESIGNER: Joan K. Morris

Raja Dish

Elephants never forget! Display this bowl near the front door, make it a habit to toss your keys in it, and you'll always remember where they are.

PAPER
Red-and-yellow checkered paper
Black-and-white checkered paper

OTHER MATERIALS
13 printed words, in any language
Image of an animal
Shallow glass dish, 5½ inches (14 cm) in diameter
Matte medium
Gold acrylic paint
Floral image
Water-based varnish
4 felt pads
Gold-colored permanent marker

TOOLS
Scissors
Ruler or tape measure
Pencil
Felt pen
Brushes
Paint scraper

NOTE: *When decoupaging onto glass, always attach the images face-down to the underside of the object unless instructed otherwise.*

WHAT YOU DO

1 Cut out the words (see the Tip). Cut 30 strips of the red-and-yellow paper, each ¼ x 1½ inches (6 mm x 3.8 cm). Cut four pieces of the black-and-white paper, each 2 x 4 inches (5.1 x 10.2 cm). Cutting short strips will make it easier to wrap the paper over the curved sides of the dish later.

2 Center the dish, right side up, over the area of the animal image you wish to have on its bottom. Trace around the bottom of the dish and cut along that line.

3 Center the animal image inside the bottom of the bowl; use the felt pen to trace its outline onto the glass. Flip the bowl upside down; on its exterior, paint matte medium inside the outline and just a bit beyond it. Place the image face down on the matte medium. Working from the center of the image out in long pulls, press out any air bubbles and extra medium. (Keep your fingers moist with medium so they don't stick to the paper.)

DESIGNER: Judy Carmichael

4 Attach all but four of the words randomly along the rim of the bowl in the manner described in step 3—you can eyeball their placement rather than marking it with a felt pen. Apply the red-and-yellow strips over them around the entire rim. Attach the remaining words at the cardinal points, perpendicular to the bottom of the dish like spokes.

5 Apply the black-and-white strips to the sides of the dish. Allow the medium to dry.

6 Paint the underside of the bowl with a coat of acrylic paint; after the paint dries, repeat. Allow it to dry completely.

7 Apply more strips of red-and-yellow checkered paper to the rim, again working on the underside of the bowl, but facing right side out. Match the ends of the strips to look like one long piece. Attach the floral image to the bottom of the bowl.

tip You could scour magazines or newspapers for text that matches your imagery—or simply come up with the words you want to use and type them into a word processing document. Experiment with font styles, sizes, and colors, then print the page to cut them out.

8 Apply four coats of varnish to the underside of the bowl. After they dry, glue the felt pads to the bottom of the bowl. Scrape away any dried glue, matte medium, or varnish that has collected on the dish's edge. Draw a line of gold along the edge of the bowl with the marking pen.

Birds Alight

Turn a discarded old window into a piece of art. When it's placed in front of sunlight, the birds become enveloped in a luminous halo.

PAPER

4 sheets of vellum

6 sheets of paper embossed with a raised paisley design

OTHER MATERIALS

Old wood-framed window

Vintage illustration of a bird

Decoupage medium

Black marker

Masking tape

Assorted beads

Small brass screw eyes

Thin fishing line

Crimp beads

Screws and chain for hanging (optional)

TOOLS

Color photocopier

Scissors or craft knife

Flat brush

Pencil

Crimping pliers

WHAT YOU DO

1 Clean and dry the windowpanes.

2 Working in sections, enlarge the illustration on the color copier so that it fills most of the window frame. Cut it out, using either scissors or a craft knife.

3 Starting at the center panels and working outward, use decoupage medium to attach the cutouts of the illustration to the *front* of the panes. Line them up carefully so the image appears to be created from one piece of paper. Whenever you reach a muntin (one of the wooden partitions that separate the windowpanes), use a finger to shape the paper so it conforms to the wood, then glue the paper to it, too. Allow the medium to dry.

DESIGNER: Diana Light

4 Use the marker to draw a rough outline around the illustration on the front of the glass. Using masking tape, label each pane with a consecutive number, starting with 1.

5 Cut vellum rectangles to the size of the panes and place them temporarily on the front of each piece of glass. Using the pencil, lightly transcribe the pane number to each piece of vellum. With light shining through the front of the window, use the pencil to trace the black marker lines drawn in step 4. Remove the vellum pieces and wipe away the marker.

6 Cut pieces from the embossed paper to the size of the windowpanes.

7 Pair a vellum rectangle with an embossed one; match up their edges and hold them together with little bits of masking tape. Using scissors, cut both pieces along the marker line traced on the vellum; set the cuttings aside in a little pile.

Repeat until you've cut all the pairs, keeping all the sets of cuttings separate.

8 Carefully remove the masking tape from the set of cuttings labeled "1." Brush decoupage medium onto the entire *back* of the windowpane with the corresponding number. Choose the vellum pieces that halo the illustration when viewed from the front, and apply them to the medium. Fill in the rest of the pane with the matching embossed cutout, placing it face down against the glass.

Repeat with the rest of the panes, and allow them to dry.

9 Determine where you wish to hang the strands of beads, and mount pairs of screw eyes in the appropriate places in the sashes and muntins. Cut pieces of fishing line and thread one through the upper screw eye of each pair. Use a crimping bead to fasten each piece of line to the hardware (see the Tip).

Arrange the beads as desired along each piece of fishing line, keeping them in place by flanking them with crimp beads. Thread each end of line through the opposite screw eye, pull the line tight, and use a crimping bead to fasten it.

10 Attach the screws and chain to the top of the window if you wish to hang it for display.

tip Most bead shops stock crimping beads in the findings section of the store. To make flat crimps, simply place a crimp bead in position and flatten it with chain-nose pliers.

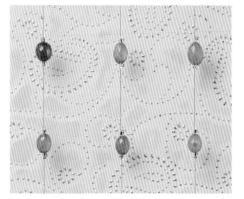

Versailles Stool

If Marie Antoinette had had access to a color photocopier, she might have tried her hand at this project. Applying scaled-down copies of the fabric to the wooden part of the stool adds a layer of interest while keeping the design visually unified.

MATERIALS

Vanity stool with cloth seat
1 yard of patterned fabric
Paint matching the fabric
Decoupage medium
Clear gloss spray sealer
1½ yards of matching trim

TOOLS

2-inch paintbrush
Color photocopier with the
    ability to enlarge and reduce
Scissors
Staple gun and staples
1-inch paintbrush
Hot glue gun

WHAT YOU DO

1 Remove the seat from the stool and take off the old fabric. Set it aside to use as a pattern later, and also keep any foam or padding on the seat. Paint the wood and allow it to dry overnight.

2 Make 20 color copies of the new fabric, reducing it to 60%. Cut out the designs.

3 Using the old fabric conserved from step 1 as your pattern, cut a piece of the new fabric. Use it to reupholster the seat, stapling it in place. Don't reattach the seat yet, but place it in position to help you decide the placement of the cutouts on the apron and legs of the stool. Nothing says you have to place the paper to mimic the fabric pattern, so have fun experimenting!

4 Working around the stool, paint medium on the back of a cutout and place it where it belongs on the stool. Rub out any bubbles and wrinkles, then paint a coat of decoupage medium over the paper. Let the medium dry overnight.

Cutting-Edge Decoupage

5 Spray the chair with the sealer, following the manufacturer's instructions. Be careful not to get any on the fabric. Let it dry, then apply another coat.

6 Using hot glue, attach the trim around the bottom of the seat.

tips Reducing at 60% worked for the cloth shown in this project, but the material you choose might work better at a different scale, so experiment with the ratio—you could even opt to enlarge your fabric instead of diminishing the size of the patterns.

Examine the motifs and overall pattern in your own fabric to see what it suggests about arranging your cutouts. In this case, the designer took inspiration from the symmetrical nature of the fabric imagery. She placed one design on the right leg, for example, with an identical design in the same location on the left leg. On the back, she placed a larger design in the center with smaller ones on either side.

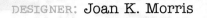

DESIGNER: Joan K. Morris

Sweet Dreams

This is an adventurous project for those who love to decorate boldly. Painting the wall and the headboard the same neutral color unifies both, creating a canvas for the decoupage.

DESIGNER: Joan K. Morris

PAPER

1 roll of wrapping paper for
    the flowers
3 sheets of cardstock for the circles
Butcher paper

OTHER MATERIALS

Flat and semi-gloss paints in
    matching colors
Wooden headboard
Scrap poster board or cardstock
Masking tape
Gloss decoupage medium
Flat finish decoupage glue
Clear gloss spray sealer
Clear flat spray sealer

TOOLS

Photocopier
Scissors
Pencil
Various brushes
Expired credit card
Craft knife
1-inch (2.5 cm) circle punch
½-inch (1.3 cm) circle punch

tip Despite the integrated, mono-
chromatic appearance of the wall and
headboard, the designer created visual
interest by using two different finishes of
paint—glossy and flat. Matching the finishes of the paint and the decoupage medium
disguises the presence of the adhesive.

WHAT YOU DO

1 Apply flat paint to the wall. Paint the
headboard with semi-gloss. Let the paint
dry overnight.

2 Using a photocopier, enlarge both flower
templates on page 96. Cut and trace them
onto scrap poster board, then cut those out to
make stiff patterns.

3 Place the headboard in position against the
wall. Trace and cut out five large flowers
and six small ones from the wrapping paper.
Arrange them on the headboard and on the
wall, using masking tape to temporarily keep
them in place; it doesn't matter whether areas
hang over the edge of the headboard. Attach
the flowers, using the gloss decoupage medium
applied to the wrong side of the paper. If any
sections overhang the edge of the headboard,
don't wrap them around it. Use a credit card
to smooth out any wrinkles and bubbles, then
paint a layer of medium over each flower.

After the medium has dried, use a craft
knife to carefully slice off the part of any flower
that extends beyond the edge of the furniture,
closely following the headboard's outline, and
save the cut-off piece.

4 Use the 1-inch hole punch to make 60
circles from the cardstock.

5 With the headboard in position, tack one
circle in the bottom center of each flower
with masking tape. Using more masking tape,
temporarily attach pieces of butcher paper

the wall and the headboard, placing them between the flowers wherever you wish to create stems. Lightly sketch twig shapes directly onto the butcher paper. Untape the butcher paper and cut out the twigs.

6 Remove the circles from the flower centers. Using decoupage medium applied to the wrong side of the butcher paper, attach the stems. If portions of the stem overhang the edge of the headboard, don't wrap them around it. Rub away any wrinkles.

Paint a coat of medium over the stems; use gloss medium on the headboard, and flat on the wall. After the medium has dried, use a craft knife to carefully slice away any parts of the stems that extend beyond the headboard's edge, carefully following the headboard's outline. Save the cut-off pieces.

7 Glue down the circles in the flower centers. Paint a coat of medium over each.

8 With the headboard in position, experiment with the composition of the remaining circles on the headboard and the wall, using masking tape to hold them in place. Once you have a pleasing arrangement, glue them down one at a time, painting the back with glue and returning it to its place. (Remember, use gloss medium on the headboard, and flat on the wall.) After gluing them all down, paint a coat of medium over each one.

9 Use the ½-inch punch to make 65 brown paper dots. Follow the instructions in step 8 to arrange and glue them into place.

10 With the headboard in place, use masking tape to arrange the cut-off pieces saved from steps 3 and 6 on the wall, lining them up to match with their other halves on the headboard. Glue them down, using flat decoupage medium. Allow the medium to dry.

11 Following the manufacturer's instructions, spray two coats of gloss sealer on the headboard. Spray the areas of the wall with decoupage on them with flat sealer. Allow it to dry completely.

Nippon Box

This delicate box is in the Japanese *maki-e* style, which translates as "seed picture." It features an innovative technique that uses a home ink-jet printer to reproduce classical Japanese imagery onto sheets prepared with imitation metal leaf.

DESIGNER: Pamela Cowdery Franceschetto

PAPER

Printer paper

Single-sided metallic origami paper

Japanese rice paper or washi paper

OTHER MATERIALS

Unfinished wooden box

Putty

Wet/dry sandpaper in 280, 320,
and 400 grits

Gesso

Black acrylic paint

0000 steel wool

Water-based polyurethane varnish

Masking tape

Tinted metallic mica powders in
bronze, deep gold, and light gold

Metallic gold acrylic paint

Water-based sizing

Imitation gold leaf in gold, copper,
and silver

Transparent acrylic spray

Digital images of Japanese clip-art
drawings

PVA glue

Mother-of-pearl sheet (see Tip
under step 6)

Tracing paper

Acrylic wallpaper glue

Water

Paper towels

Micro-mesh polishing kit

Mild liquid dishwashing detergent

Furniture paste wax

TOOLS

Assorted brushes

Old toothbrush

Ink-jet printer

Pencil

Curved nail scissors

Files for artificial fingernails

Rubber roller

Cotton rag

NOTE: *When creating a complex decoupage project such as this one, apply a coat of varnish after each step. It will preserve the work beneath it; if one of the steps turns out not to your liking, you just have to remove and complete that step, not the entire project.*

WHAT YOU DO

1 Fill any holes or imperfections in the box with putty. Allow it to harden, then sand the box, inside and out, until smooth.

Apply several coats of acrylic gesso to the exterior of the box, letting each coat dry completely. Sand, using 320-grit sandpaper moistened slightly to form a slurry as you work. Repeat as necessary until the surface of the box is absolutely smooth and without imperfections.

2 Apply several light coats of black paint, letting each coat dry completely. Sand the box lightly with dry 400-grit paper. Apply a final coat of paint diluted with water. Let it dry, then lightly sand it with steel wool to create a smooth, matte finish.

Apply a coat of varnish to protect the surface.

3 Use masking tape to cover the areas of the box that you wish to remain black.

Add water to each of the mica powders; the mixture should have the consistency of whipping cream.

Create the speckled finish by using the toothbrush to lightly spatter each color onto the box, working from the darkest shade to the lightest.

Paint the edges of the lid with gold acrylic paint. Let it dry. Remove the masking tape, and apply a coat of varnish. Set the box aside.

4 Apply water-based sizing to sheets of printer paper. Following the manufacturer's instructions, after the sizing becomes tacky, apply the imitation leaf. Let the sheets dry overnight or longer.

Using a soft brush, gently brush away excess leaf. Apply several light coats of acrylic spray to protect the foil and prevent it from oxidizing. Allow the paper to dry for at least 24 hours.

5 Print the digital images directly onto the foil-prepared sheets. Wait a few minutes, then apply two or three light coats of acrylic spray. Allow to dry completely. Cut out the images and set them aside.

> **tip** With most home ink-jet printers, the printed images must be sealed using either transparent acrylic spray or clear shellac to prevent the colors from running when gluing and varnishing. This is not necessary with heavy-duty laser printers or color photocopiers. When in doubt, immerse a printed cutout in water to test its colorfastness.

6 Glue the mother-of-pearl pieces to the sheets of metallic origami paper—the color underneath the shell will determine the shade of its final appearance. Let the glue dry completely for one or two days.

Working from a print-out of your imagery, determine which parts of the design you wish to replace with mother-of-pearl. Using tracing paper, transfer these to the back of the mother-of-pearl. Carefully cut them out, using short snips of the nail scissors. File the edges smooth.

> **tip** You might look for mother-of-pearl in sheet form through stores or catalogs that sell guitar-making supplies, fine woodworking materials, or items for jewelry making. You'll definitely find a large array of it online in gorgeous patterns and dyed in eye-popping colors; perform a search using the term "mother-of-pearl veneer."

7 Mix up an adhesive that's three parts glue, one part wallpaper glue, and one part water.

8 Compose the cutouts from step 5 on the box, mixing and matching the different metals to highlight the design elements. Cut away the details that you plan to replace with the mother-of-pearl.

Glue down a cutout, place a damp paper towel over it, and use a small rubber roller to press out air bubbles. Attach the rest of the cutouts in the same fashion, then glue the mother-of-pearl details into place. Allow to dry 24 to 48 hours.

Check for loose edges or air bubbles, then coat the entire object with white polymer glue. Allow it to dry completely.

9 Apply 20 coats of varnish, brushing each on in alternate directions. Follow the manufacturer's instructions for drying times between coats.

10 Sand the box, first using 280-grit paper dipped in water with a squirt of detergent. Use a regular, back-and-forth motion over small sections, repeating until the entire object has been sanded. Immediately repeat the process with 320-grit paper. Rinse the box and let it dry at least 24 hours.

11 Apply five more coats of varnish. Sand the box, employing the same procedure as in step 10 but using 400-grit paper. Rinse the box and let it dry.

Repeat this procedure until the box becomes perfectly smooth and you can no longer feel the thickness of the mother-of-pearl. Allow the box to dry completely.

12 Lightly rub the box with steel wool until it's no longer shiny. Polish the box using a micro-mesh kit of graded polishing sponges dipped in soapy water. After polishing is complete, wash the box and let it dry.

13 Apply paste wax to the box with a wet rag. After it dries, buff it with a soft polishing cloth.

14 Finish the interior of the box by cutting the rice or washi paper to the size of each panel and gluing it into place.

About the Designers

When **Judy Carmichael** decided to revamp an old rusty tray 10 years ago, she searched for guidance from some books on decoupage. One of them contained a small section on decoupage under glass, and she was so smitten by the lustrous appearance of the finished product that she got completely sidetracked. She only overhauled the tray three years later! Judy holds a teaching degree from Althouse College at The University of Western Ontario. She taught French for several years before narrowing her focus to family and art. Judy decoupages on glass in her one-person studio and also holds workshops for small groups at her homes in Collingwood and London, Ontario, Canada. She lives with her husband and their three school-age children.

Pamela Cowdery Franceschetto is a New Englander by birth and temperament, but her Italian husband swept her away to the sunny Mediterranean 20 years ago. Some time ago, feeling the need to create something with her hands but not gifted at drawing, she gravitated to decoupage—it seemed easy since it was "just" cutting and pasting. Since then, she has geared her efforts toward bringing classical decoupage technique into the 21st century. Pamela lives near Parma, Italy, and is currently president of Découpage Italia, the Italian association of decoupage.

Colette George is a passionate designer, decorator, and the author of her own decoupage book. Among other clients, Colette designs for a major paint company. To learn more about her work, visit www.colettedesigns.net.

Wendi Gratz makes many things. She designs quilts, jewelry, clothing, dolls, and furniture—always striving for functionality as well as beauty. Whenever possible, she tries to recycle, reuse, and refashion. For this book, she was happy to make over a particularly ugly filing cabinet that had been hanging around her office for years. Her work appears in *Simple Contemporary Quilts* (Lark Books, 2007). She maintains a website at www.wendigratz.com.

Steven James has played with macaroni, glitter, and glue since he was a child. He resides in San Francisco where he operates macaroniandglitter.com, a website devoted to creative living. In addition to teaching around the country, Steven has also appeared as a designer on the HGTV and DIY networks. His work has been published in *ReadyMade* magazine and *Extreme Office Crafts* (Lark Books, 2007), as well as in various newspapers and websites. Contact the designer at stevenjames@macaroniandglitter.com.

Marthe LeVan is an acquisitions editor for Lark Books, with a specialty in jewelry and metal. Since 2000, she has written, edited, and designed projects for more books than she can count on all her fingers and toes.

Diana Light is a d-light-ful artist who has the uncanny ability to make everything she touches look absolutely fabulous and instantly cool. She's the author of *The Weekend Crafter: Etching Glass* (Lark Books, 2000), and has also made projects for a number of other Lark titles; her most recent creations appear in *The Michael's Book of Paper Crafts* (2005) and *Hip Handbags* (2005). Contact Diana at dianalight@hotmail.com.

Nicole Novak Luperini is a collage and mixed-media artist. She holds a degree in Biology and Studio Art from Hood College in Frederick, Md., and now works in interior design. Her passion for fabric, color, texture, and natural elements combines a love of interiors with her fascination for biology. Nicole's work has been published in *Stamping with Style* (Lark Books, 2001), as well as in various magazines. Nicole lives in Burbank, Calif. with her husband, two cats, and a dog. She is currently creating a website at www.siennamoon.com, and can be reached at siennamoondesigns@yahoo.com.

Joan K. Morris's artistic endeavors have led her down many successful creative paths, including ceramics and costume design for motion pictures. Joan has contributed projects for numerous Lark books, including *Creative Stitching on Paper* (2006), *Exquisite Embellishments for Your Clothes* (2006), *Beautiful Ribbon Crafts* (2003), *Gifts For Baby* (2004), *Hardware Style* (2004), and *Hip Handbags* (2005).

LuAnne Payne has loved all things crafty and art-related for as long as she can remember. She most enjoys making pieces that are whimsical, uplifting, and nostalgic. A packrat at heart, she tries to give her work a retro feel by incorporating bits from her collection of vintage papers. She lives in North Carolina with her husband, two children, and a dog. Find more of her work at silverymoonart.etsy.com.

Terry Taylor is the author of several Lark Books including *Altered Art* (2005), *Artful Paper Dolls* (2006), and *The Altered Object* (2006). When he's not working on books or projects for Lark Books, he's a mixed-media artist and jeweler. He has studied jewelry and metal work at John C. Campbell Folk School, Appalachian Center for Crafts, and Haystack Mountain School of Crafts.

Templates

All Aflutter, page 70.
Enlarge to desired size.

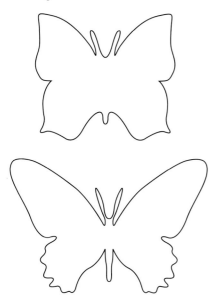

Sweet Dreams, page 88.
Enlarge to desired size.

Index